A Biblical Guide on Leadership
LUD GOLZ

A cataloguing record for this book that includes the U.S. Library of Congress Classification number, the Library of Congress Call number and the Dewey Decimal cataloguing code is available from the National Library of Cananda. The complete cataloguing record can be obtained from the National Library's online database at: www.nlc-bnc.ca/amicus/index-e.html
ISBN: 1-4120-1698-3

TRAFFORD

This book was published *on-demand* in cooperation with Trafford Publishing.
On-demand publishing is a unique process and service of making a book available for retail sale to the public taking advantage of on-demand manufacturing and Internet marketing. *On-demand* publishing includes promotions, retail sales, manufacturing, order fulfilment, accounting and collecting royalties on behalf of the author.

Suite 6E, 2333 Government St., Victoria, **B.C. V8T 4P4, CANADA**
Phone   250-383-6864   Toll-free   1-888-232-4444 (Canada & US)
Fax   250-383-6804   E-mail   sales@trafford.com
Web site: www.trafford.com TRAFFORD PUBLISHING IS A DIVISION OF TRAFFORD HOLDINGS LTD.
Trafford Catalogue #03-2075 **www.trafford.com/robots/03-2075.html**

10   9   8   7   6   5   4   3   2   1

Printed and bound in India by
Authentic India, Secunderabd 500 003
E-mail: printing@ombooks.org

A Biblical Guide on Leadership
LUD GOLZ

TABLE OF CONTENTS

INTRODUCTION

YOU CAN MAKE THINGS HAPPEN

Yes, you can.

All of us have tremendous potential to be used of God to make things happen.

Paul declared, "I can do anything through Him who gives me strength" (Philippians 4:13, Williams). Paul obviously made things happen. But when things happened he made it clear who was to get the credit: "By the grace of God I am what I am (and it could be said, 'I do what I do'), and His grace to me was not without effect. No, I worked harder than all of them – yet not I, but the grace of God that was with me" (1 Corinthians 15:10).

Nehemiah confessed the same truth when he wrote after completing the building of the wall around Jerusalem that even their enemies "realized that this work had been done with the help of our God" (Nehemiah 6:15-16).

This book presents Biblical guidelines for leadership discovered through a study of the book of Nehemiah. Nehemiah did great things for God. He demonstrated guidelines which enabled him to make things happen. He was not perfect. But we can learn from his strengths and weaknesses, successes and failures.

My prayer is that what you learn from this study will motivate and enable you to make things happen for God's glory and the benefit of many in your world. Apply these

Biblical guidelines for leadership. As you do I'm confident
God will use you to make things happen to further His cause.

I want to thank the believers of Fellowship Bible Church who
have encouraged and joined me as Senior Pastor for over 25
years and now as Minister at Large in making things happen
for God in our community and world.

Lud Golz, Minister at Large
Fellowship Bible Church
16391 Chillicothe Road
Chagrin Falls Ohio 44023
Email : ludgolz@aol.com

Chapter 1
HOW TO TAKE THE INITIATIVE

"If you could choose your circumstances and were not afraid of failure, what would you attempt to do for God?" (Dr. Jerry Kirk).

If it is worthwhile, why not attempt it, even if you cannot change your circumstances?

I remember counseling a middle-aged couple who wanted to plan for their future. They were having great difficulty. The more we talked it became obvious to me they were having such a hard time because they ordered their lives by focusing on the circumstances which confronted them. Seldom did they sit down and ask, "What do I want to accomplish in the next week? Month? Year?" And when they did, circumstances often sidetracked their efforts or depressed their motivation to even try. The fear of future circumstances blurs our vision and frustrates our planning.

It's true, some people go a long way by merely reacting to circumstances. They happen to be at the right place at the right time with the talent or resources to buy up the opportunity. But the vast majority of us feel trapped by our circumstances. We try to make the best of it, but down deep inside we have a lot of unfulfilled desires which are not considered because of the circumstances.

Does God only want us to react to our circumstances? Or does He want us to be initiators, making opportunities for ourselves, in spite of our circumstances?

There are times you must react to what is going on around you no matter what you were planning to initiate. But there are other times you should take the initiative and do what needs doing. When reading Nehemiah chapters 1-2 you will discover how Nehemiah took the initiative in spite of his circumstances.

Nehemiah was a layman, cupbearer to the king, who feared God and lived for Him. He was living in Susa as an exile during the time Artaxerxes was king of Persia. His homeland was devastated by the Babylonians and Jerusalem lay in shambles for a century or so. Periodically he heard reports of how poorly things were going in Palestine. Gradually a burden developed in his heart to do something positive to bring glory to God and encouragement to his people. **But the circumstances…**

Yes, the circumstances would dictate to most that nothing worthwhile could be done, especially while trapped in Susa. But Nehemiah responded differently. He demonstrated how to take the initiative.

First, he kept informed. When one of his brothers, Hanani, came from a trip to Judah, Nehemiah questioned him about how the Jewish remnant who survived the exile was doing. He also asked questions about the conditions of Jerusalem (Nehemiah 1:2). Keeping informed of conditions is critical for planning to do something about them.

This takes time. To many it seems as though it is unproductive time. Often it appears to be wasted time. But persistence here always pays off in the long run.

I will never forget reading about Thomas Edison, the great inventor. Once, after many experiments had failed, he was asked, "Don't you get discouraged by all these failures?"

"Discouraged," he replied. "Not at all. I know a few hundred approaches that won't work!"

One of the great needs in the church is for Christians to become better informed about the needs and opportunities in the world. The term "world Christian" is being used for those who become informed about what is going on in the world and sensitized to their potential to make things happen.

Many churches have no active Missions Committee. And many who do, do little to help them become informed, so they can provide enlightened leadership to the church's involvement in the world. Many agencies have staff and literature to help in this. We must become better informed or the vision for impacting our world will never crystallize and the church will die. "Without a vision the people perish" (Proverbs 29:18 KJV).

Nehemiah's relentless research crystallized the picture of need in his mind. Hanani's report triggered a deep response in his heart. When he heard that the survivors were in great trouble and disgrace and that the wall of Jerusalem was broken down with the gates burned, he "sat down and wept" (Nehemiah 1:4). **He identified with the need** as though he was on the scene. He felt the great trouble and disgrace as much as the survivors in Judah – maybe more. This is what it means to "weep with them who weep" (Romans 12:15).

Dr. Paul Cho, pastor of the world's largest church in Seoul, Korea, talks about becoming pregnant with a vision and carrying it until it is born. Conception takes place when getting informed overwhelms you to identify with the need.

Nehemiah's identification with the need led to his **faithful intercessory prayer for the need to be met.** "For some days I mourned and fasted and prayed before the God of heaven. Then I said…O Lord, let your ear be attentive to the prayer of this your servant and to the prayer of your servants who delight in revering your name. Give your servant success

today by granting him favor in the presence of this man"
(Nehemiah 1:4-11).

I like the boldness of Nehemiah when he prayed, "Give your
servant success **today.**"

Did God answer his request on that first day? No. The next
day? No. Four months later the answer came. I can see and
hear Nehemiah praying daily for four long months, "Give
your servant success **today.**"

Once research has crystallized a vision in your heart of what
God wants and you identify with it wholeheartedly, then
pray faithfully until the vision is implemented. Often, during
those days of waiting, as you seek God's face, the vision will
be clarified. God knows best when you are ready and when
circumstances are best.

William Carey was a cobbler, but he studied diligently the
spiritual needs of the world. After much research and prayer
as well as rebuff from a group of ministers he wrote a treatise
titled, "An Inquiry Into The Obligations Of Christians To Use
Means For The Conversion Of The Heathen." In God's time
this became a catalyst which not only got him to India where
he did a great work for God, but also opened the door to the
modern missionary movement.

On the day God's time came to answer Nehemiah's prayer the king inquired about his sad countenance (Nehemiah 2:1-2) Evidently Nehemiah had kept his burden to himself and God. But when the right time came he was ready to share it with the king and ask permission to carry out his vision. "And because the gracious hand of my God was upon me, the king granted my request" (Nehemiah 2:8).

While waiting for God's answer Nehemiah continued faithfully serving the king as cupbearer. Sometimes remaining faithful in present responsibilities is the most difficult aspect in this waiting period.

He also prayerfully sharpened his ideas on how to carry out his vision for Jerusalem. Then when the opportunity came he was ready to spell out his goals as well as what he would need to realize those goals.

Often I have ideas about what I'd like to do. But while I wait for God's time, rather than developing and sharpening the plan so it can be implemented when God's time comes, I'm preoccupied with other things.

Nehemiah was ready when the time came. This reminds me of the apostle Paul who once declared he was ready to preach the gospel to those in Rome (Romans 1:12-16). **Am I ready to initiate what is on my heart?**

I will be if I keep informed, identify with the need or opportunity, and faithfully pray about it. I will also be better as a reactor should my circumstances change. God wants us to be ready to buy up each opportunity He puts before us and burdens us to tackle (Ephesians 5:16).

One of the most unusual and fulfilling experiences I had as a young man took place during my junior year at the Moody Bible Institute. For two years I did not have a break from either study, work or summer Christian service. I was sensing a real need for a break, a change of pace, a rest.

Beginning around November I made a daily practice to get on my knees at my bed with a wall map of North America before me. I would begin praying, "Father, you know how exhausted I am. I need a change of pace. Next summer I would like to go somewhere where I could work just enough to pay my expenses. The rest of the time I would like to rest and read and be refreshed. I don't know where you would have me go, but please show me..."

Then as I scanned the North American continent before me, for some reason my eyes focused on Churchill, Manitoba, Canada. It is a small northern port town on the Hudson Bay through which they ship grain to Europe for the two months the northern route is unfrozen.

I didn't know why, but once my eyes focused on Churchill
each day I was overcome and would break down in tears as
I prayed for God to work in that town. I was not able to be
more specific in my prayers because I knew almost nothing
about the place.

After a month of this daily experience I felt I should try to
find out what I could about why I had this tremendous burden
for Churchill. I went to Ken Taylor, then director of Moody
Press and now better known as the translator and publisher
of the Living Bible. I asked him if he knew anyone I could
contact in Churchill. He gave me some names of missions
that worked in the remote areas of northern Canada. I wrote
them and waited for their response.

Nothing happened. No one replied. But I still broke down as
I prayed for Churchill. Gradually the burden began to fade.

Months later a missionary from one of the missions I had
written came to Moody and looked me up. As we talked he
shared two amazing things. First, he said the missionaries
who served in that region were going through a severe time of
what they thought was a Satanic attack during the past winter.
Second, they were looking for some college kids to come to
Churchill to help them in their work for the summer.

Guess who went? And guess who persuaded a close friend to go?

It was a true change of pace. I worked hard but had plenty of time for relaxation in this remote area of northern Canada. God drew me very close to Himself, even as He used me and my friend to help the missionaries in the work of Christ there. It was an experience I will never forget.

Application Assignment:

1. If circumstances did not hinder you and you were not afraid of failure, state what you would like to do with your life.
2. List the circumstances which hinder you from doing this.
3. Identify the reasons for any fear of failure you have.
4. How much research have you done related to what you would like to do? Have you talked to anyone who knows specific facts related to the project? Do you know anyone who might have such facts?
5. Has your interest in this project intensified or waned with time?
6. Can you visualize in your mind's eye what the project, if accomplished, would look like? Describe it in one paragraph.
7. Have you prayed specifically and faithfully about things related to the project?

8. Are your prayers for the project's realization offered in a spirit of urgency? (Remember Nehemiah prayed "today").

9. Are you more ready today to tackle the project than you were a few weeks or months or even years ago? Do you have a clearer understanding of what is involved? (Remember Moses waited 40 years).

10. Is the project worthwhile enough for you to wait for the right time to see it materialize?

Chapter 2
CREATIVE PERSEVERANCE

It was Francoise Pasqualini who once declared:

> "Know what you want.
>> Find out what it takes to get it.
>> Act on it.
>> Persevere!"

The last step – **perseverance** – is the most difficult of these
four steps for most of us. It is the discipline which separates
the men from the boys, the achievers from the attempters,
those who finish from those who also ran.

John Akjwan of Tanzania represented his country in the 26
mile marathon in the Mexican Olympics. Early in the race
he slipped and severely injured himself, suffering many cuts.
There was a fair amount of bleeding. He did the best job he
could with help that was available to bandage the wounds.
Then he started to run again.

The race was won by Mamo Wolde of Ethiopia. After the
rest of the runners had crossed the finish line and the crowd
had all but left John Akjwan finally entered the arena,
struggling and in much pain with each step he took. When
he crossed the finish line the first aid workers who were still

there quickly assisted him to a stretcher and began treating his wounds. As they were caring for him one of them asked him why he kept on running when he knew he would not win or even place in the race.

John Akjwan responded resolutely, "My country didn't send me here to start the race. They sent me here to finish the race!"

He understood what perseverance is all about.

It takes a lot of work to get a vision crystallized and on the road. But usually it is even harder to keep it going. More people need to be involved and unexpected obstacles need to be overcome. Keeping on target is not easy. And maintaining or building momentum can become very difficult.

The Church I served as Senior Pastor since its founding passed the 25 year milestone a few years ago. I am now the Minister at Large, serving together with my successor. There was much excitement during the early years. The vision was simple. Organization was minimal. Costs were low. Potential was great.

God has been faithful, but it has not been easy. A good number of our people moved to other parts of the country.

New folk replaced them, but they often had a different
perspective of our ministry. Needs among our people
changed. As we moved toward building our own facility we
encountered obstacles. Operating costs skyrocketed when we
moved into the finished building.

Getting started was difficult. But continuing what was
started, keeping it moving toward established goals, has been
even more difficult. A decade ago, while considering adding
to our facility, we decided to launch a branch church instead.
We wanted them to have a strong start so we sent out close
to 100 of our people, including four leaders and a seasoned
professional who became their pastor. That was exciting
but it required a new beginning for us. Now, under our new
Senior Pastor we have launched a new expansion project. I
have found great encouragement and help from studying
Nehemiah's creative perseverance (Nehemiah 2:11-5:19).

Nehemiah didn't waste time once he got to Jerusalem
(Nehemiah 2:11-16). He immediately did some on sight
research to confirm in person the research he had gathered
second hand while in Susa. He wanted to be sure of his facts
so he could present his challenge clearly and convincingly to
the people.

With this final review behind him he informed the people of
the vision he had to rebuild Jerusalem's walls. In this initial

session he described the condition of the walls, delivered
the challenge to rebuild, and declared his confidence in
God to give them success (Nehemiah 2:17-20). Being this
well prepared in heart and mind it is not surprising that the
people's response was, "Let us start rebuilding"
(Nehemiah 2:18).

Not wasting any time he immediately **recruited the people
and assigned responsibilities.** It didn't matter what their
vocation or position was in society. Willingness to build
qualified them to participate. All the way from the high
priest and his fellow priests to temple servants, along with
merchants, goldsmiths, perfume makers and rulers, they
joined hands to rebuild the wall (Nehemiah 3).

Each group of people under designated leaders was given a
section of the wall to repair, including the gates. Nehemiah
knew what needed to be done and how much available
manpower would be required to complete the task. Job
descriptions were simple but thorough enough to pull it all
together.

Sometimes we can make things happen by ourselves. More
often we need to share the vision and recruit fellow workers.
Then we must spell out not only the overall goal, but also the
specific goals each individual or group is responsible for.

Don't be surprised, however, when some who agreed to the

overall goal, renege when assigned a specific goal.
Accountability often exposes half-hearted commitment. It is
to the credit of the men of Tekoa that they carried out their
assignment even though "their nobles would not put their
shoulders to the work under their supervisors"
(Nehemiah 3:5). There are "sour grapes" in every group.

If the enemy or opposition can't discourage us from within
they will launch attacks from without. At first the approach
might be a subtle taunt, eg. "What are these feeble Jews
doing? Will they restore their walls?...Can they bring the
stones back to life from these heaps of rubble – burned as
they are?...What they are building – if even a fox climbed up
on it, he would break down their wall of stones!"(Nehemiah
4:2-3).

How should you respond to such taunts? Is it best to ignore
them? Maybe some would remain unaffected. But most
people get worn down by such innuendoes. Our opposition
is often a master at sowing seeds of discouragement. And
discouragement if unchecked spreads like weeds.

Nehemiah's spiritual instincts immediately drove him to God
in prayer (Nehemiah 4:4-5). His prayer is not a model of
compassion. He didn't mince words with God. He wanted
those who were attempting to discourage them wiped out,
then and there!

He didn't pray that the workers would keep from becoming discouraged. They had momentum going with them. He attacked the enemy head on, seeking to cut him off at the pass. "So we rebuilt the wall till all of it reached half its height, for the people worked with all their heart" (Nehemiah 4:6).

The opposition didn't give up readily. They regrouped and plotted to stir up trouble against the work by launching a surprise attack.

Nehemiah now had all the people pray as well as **post a guard** day and night. But these efforts were not enough. They began saying, "The strength of the laborers is giving out, and there is so much rubble that we cannot rebuild the wall" (Nehemiah 4:10). They began to believe the earlier taunts.

Such rumors are lethal. There was more rubble when they started the project, but in their eyes the rubble heaps were getting bigger and bigger. Something had to be done. And soon.

Nehemiah didn't want to stop the work. He didn't want to lose momentum. But he had to **realistically reevaluate his strategy.** There were some weak spots in the wall which made them vulnerable to the enemy. He positioned the families of those responsible for those sections right at the weak spots. This heightened their vulnerability but it also gave them greater reason to work harder and stay more alert. They also were given arms to protect themselves.

In addition he armed half the men while the other half worked on the wall. And those who worked carried materials with one hand and held a weapon in the other. Those who worked with both hands had their weapons at their side.

Though all were still accountable for their section of the wall, in the case of an attack a trumpet would sound and all were to go to the point of need and help defend it. These and other adjustments drew the people together. And this in turn spurred them on. In fact, they became so involved they didn't even take time to change clothes.

The ultimate goal never changed. The strategy for reaching that goal was changed as needed. And always, under-girding the work, Nehemiah maintained, "Our God will fight for us!" (Nehemiah 4:20).

Yet, while he led the people in this great project he remained sensitive to the needy among them. Times of crisis can be times of opportunity for the advantaged while being times of oppression for the disadvantaged. Nehemiah did all he could to equalize the burden as well as the opportunity. Most important he, as the governor, didn't take advantage of his position at the expense of the people. He shared freely from his own resources.

Everything was designed to complete the project.
Everyone had the privilege of participating. And no one was allowed to profit at the expense of others. In this way momentum and motivation would be maintained at a high level.

This was creative perseverance at its best.

Application Assignment

1. Are you engaged in a project which means very much to you? Describe it in a few sentences specifying the basic goals of the project.
2. Do you have measurable objectives which when completed result in achieving the basic goal? List the measurable objectives in order of priority.
3. Have you or will you need to enlist the assistance of others? If yes, do you have a job description worked out for them that is specific enough for them to know what their contribution will be toward reaching the basic goal of the project? If you don't have such a job description, prepare one.
4. Have you encountered opposition either in the form of

taunts or outright assaults?   Explain. How have you responded?

5. Has such opposition kept you from persevering in your intention of realizing the desired goal? If so, what are you going to do about it?

6. How would you describe your prayer life as a way of attacking the problem?

7. Have you or do you think you would be wise in considering some changes in your strategy to reach the desired goal? Explain.

8. Have you ignored the welfare of some of your people in order to move forward toward achieving your goal? What can you do to correct this?

9. Have you made a concerted effort to include others in the process of planning, including goals and strategy? And have you made an effort to train   someone or a number of others to be able to take over should something happen to you?

Chapter 3
WHEN I'M INTIMIDATED –
A RESPONSE STRATEGY

It's not that everyone wants to totally control a pastor. It's just that some church people and board members want the pastor to do things their way – regardless.

Sometimes it's bearable. Sometimes.

I will never forget one board meeting in my first pastorate. I was finishing my last year of college. In the United States on a student visa, I was not allowed to work any more than twenty hours each week.

Before I started my service there, I had explained my legal limitations and assured them that, at times of real need, I'd be willing to work extra hours to meet that need.

At this particular board meeting they confronted me with a list of complaints. The first was that I'd not been putting in anywhere close to forty hours a week, while asking them to sacrifice for the Lord. The final one was a conclusion. They did not feel I was qualified for the pastorate!

With some fear and suppressed frustration, I explained again my legal limitations on work hours. I apologized for not

making myself clearer at the outset of our relationship. I
affirmed my conviction that God indeed had called me into
His work, and I renewed my commitment to them.

It was a hard experience, one that could have turned me not
only out of the ministry but against it. But my wife and
I stayed there for two more years. Though we didn't see
significant growth in the church, God did do some wonderful
things in the lives of the people and in our lives as well.
During those years I wrote my first two books.

I have since found help and encouragement from studying the
life of Nehemiah, who faced formidable odds when he rebuilt
Jerusalem's walls. After making thorough preparation,
rallying the people to participate, and getting involved in the
work, he was confronted by unspiritual people who viewed
his work in a negative light.

Being a great leader he had **a response strategy** that helped
him recognize and gain the victory over intimidation. It
is clearly illustrated in chapter 6 of his book. And it is a
strategy I find meets my needs today.

The first element is the **ability to detect what leads to
intimidation.** "When word came to Sanballat (and) Tobiah
that I had rebuilt the wall and not a gap was left in it…(they)
sent me this message: 'Come, let us meet together in one of

the villages on the plain of Ono'" (Nehemiah 6:1-2).
How did Nehemiah interpret their request? He evaluated
their ground rules and determined they wanted the home field
advantage.

In a wrestling match, my sons have the advantage over me.
They intimidate me physically. But if they challenge me to a
golf game, I get the advantage. A golf course is my turf.

When a pastor has prominent or influential or unspiritual
members on his board, he might be tempted to defer to their
suggestions even though they might need to be challenged by
his vision.

I think of what might have happened had William Carey, the
father of modern missions, listened when his critics declared,
"Young man, sit down. If God wants to convert the heathen,
He can do it without your help."

After four attempts by the opposition, Nehemiah's antagonists
added a new twist. They threatened to send a letter to the
king, accusing the Israelites of plotting a revolt once the wall
was built. This was not true. Nehemiah knew this. So did
the opposition. But would the king?

The second element in the strategy is **the ability to discern
truth from falsehood.**

Sometimes an accusation's falsehood is not apparent. Once, under severe pressure I almost believed some false accusations about myself.

I made an effort to be reconciled with a member of my church who had made it known he had something against me. When I approached him, he denied it. However, he later misrepresented my effort, suggesting I was not really concerned about him.

When we face such experiences, we need to pray for wisdom (James 1:5) and then evaluate the charge for its truthfulness. I had my wife listen in on the second conversation I had with this man so that she could verify what was said by both of us. Never let lies get the best of you even though they hurt. Nehemiah knew "they were all trying to frighten us, thinking, 'their hands will get too weak for the work, and it will not be completed'"(Nehemiah 6:9).

The third element **is being alert to suggestions that you should solve a problem in a manner uncharacteristic of you and contrary to your character.**

Look at verse 10. Shemaiah, supposedly a friend, told Nehemiah of a plot to kill him and suggested he run and hide in the temple.

This raised a serious question. Would Nehemiah be more

concerned for his own safety than about leading the people on to victory? Nehemiah knew himself well. He knew that running was not an option – at least, not for him.

Either Shemaiah didn't know him well or he was hired to lead Nehemiah astray. Surely, he was not sent from God. And what he suggested would be nothing less than sin for Nehemiah.

Churches I have pastured over the years have at times experienced financial shortages. On occasion people have suggested, "Look, we're concerned about paying you first. We better not expand our outreach now when money is so tight."

If I agreed, was I projecting more concern about my salary than my church's ministry? My confidence that God would meet my needs might spark their greater trust in Him to provide for the church's ministry.

One final guideline for detecting intimidation is **to evaluate the integrity of those challenging you or** advising you. Even nobles of Judah were under oath to Tobiah, leader of the opposition (Nehemiah 6:17-19). They became his fellow travelers, stooges in his hands to hinder the work of God through intimidation. Sometimes over-solicitous friends can inadvertently be your greatest enemies.

Now, you could become paranoid if you try to apply these guidelines in every situation. But having them in mind will be a significant asset when you have that uneasy feeling that danger is just around the corner.

After detecting intimidation, notice how Nehemiah dealt with it. He found **taking the offensive the best defense.** Also, he **concentrated on his own goal.** That kept him from getting sidetracked.

Many sincere leaders have a hard time doing this because they are not sure what God wants them to do. Often they are directionless and unmotivated. They are vulnerable to the intimidation of others.

As a pastor/leader I have found I need to read Acts 6:1-4 every once in a while to keep my priorities as a pastor in focus. Most things I'm asked or expected to do are good in themselves. But some could take more time than I have and sidetrack me from giving "attention to prayer and the ministry of the word," which is my primary calling.

When Sanballat and Tobiah intensified their attack by concocting a lie, Nehemiah responded **by telling the truth and going to God in prayer.** We should likewise not be afraid to answer false accusations. But we must beware of doing battle with mere human weapons.

Nehemiah reaffirmed his utter dependence upon God. He prayed, "Now strengthen my hands" (Nehemiah 6:9). False accusations hurt deeply. They sap us of strength. Sometimes we might wonder if it is worth going on any more. At such times, I must pray fervently and pointedly. I've learned to ask for exactly what I need – strength to go on.

David Brainerd declared, "When you feel least like praying, that is precisely when you need to pray most."

Another element of Nehemiah's response strategy was **his ability to say "No."** Many problems for all God's people arise at this point; and, unfortunately, many leaders fail here too.

Nehemiah did not have that weakness. When sorely oppressed, he prayed to God for help; and he determined to go on building the wall until it was finished. This doggedness rallied the people to diligence. "The wall was completed…in fifty-two days" (Nehemiah 6:15).

Seldom do we finish a significant project without drawing a second wind. God often allows us to be driven to our knees. He is not only our Strength. He is our reserve Source of energy.

Though I find it hard to do when I attempt something for Him, I try to make sure it is so big that only God's active involvement can accomplish it.

You would think that Nehemiah's problems were over when the wall was completed. But the attack continued. He found further disciplines necessary if he was to preserve victory over intimidation.

Like Nehemiah, we must **beware of compromise when we are threatened.** We don't want to exchange God's best for that which is merely good or expedient.

Tobiah had succeeded in intimidating many of the nobles of Judah. They would try to persuade Nehemiah that Tobiah was a nice guy. Then they would report Nehemiah's reaction back to Tobiah. Tobiah would take this information and write intimidating letters.

But Nehemiah stood firm on his convictions. He refused to compromise.

We must also **beware of complacency after victory.**

I sometimes sense myself relaxing after completing a successful activity for God. It is so easy to bask in success. But it is also dangerous. Complacency is a killer.

Realizing this danger, Nehemiah appointed gatekeepers, singers, and Levites. Then he put a God-fearing man of integrity in charge of Jerusalem and another as commander of the citadel. To these he gave instructions that would provide safety for the city (Nehemiah 7:1-3).

A former U.S. president wrote once that the hardest part of a crisis is preparation for it; the easiest part is the crisis itself; the most dangerous is the time immediately following a crisis. That is when you let down your guard.

Leaders also need to **beware of pride** – taking the glory for things God enables us to accomplish. We should always seek to do our work in such a way, that everyone will realize "that this work had been done with the help of our God" (Nehemiah 6:16).

God is a jealous God who will not share His glory with another.

Nehemiah's response strategy was eminently successful over all the enemies; attempts to intimidate him. Master his strategy and you will be better prepared to respond when facing intimidation in your daily walk.

Application Assignment

1. When was the last time you felt someone tried to intimidate you?
2. How do you feel you handled it? If you had to face it again, would you do anything differently? What?
3. Have you had a response strategy which you readily followed in the past? If so, describe it in outline form.
4. Have you ever sensed after an encounter with someone that they thought some things about you which you do not feel are true reflections of who you are? How might you better respond so that you reveal the kind of person you really are?
5. Do you get sidetracked easily? What can you do to correct this tendency?
6. Do you have a hard time saying, "No," when you know you shouldn't take on something more? What will be necessary for you to develop the ability to know when to say, "No," and when to say "Yes"?
7. What in considering Nehemiah's response strategy did you find most enlightening?

Chapter 4
CELEBRATING ACCOMPLISHMENTS

I must confess that one of my greatest weaknesses is not to celebrate accomplishments, especially the accomplishments of others. I guess my tendency is to feel that if it was genuinely done for God, He will notice and remember and reward. It is more an oversight than a reasoned response. I have thought of what Jesus said in Luke 17:7-10 about servants, that when they have done what they were asked to do, that is what is expected, and they shouldn't look for anything in return. But for me that was more a rationalization. I was wrong.

Leaders should plan for and initiate times of thanksgiving and praise, rejoicing and celebrating. These times are not only to honor God. They are therapeutic and invigorating to the participants. I believe God is greatly pleased when He sees His people rejoicing with great joy. Surely this is why He commands us to "Rejoice with those who rejoice" (Romans 12:15).

Nehemiah took great care in planning for the dedication of the wall of Jerusalem (Nehemiah 12:27-47). Building the wall against all the odds, obstacles and opposition was a significant accomplishment. And completing it in just 52 days made the accomplishment even greater. There indeed

was reason for the people of God to celebrate.
The first step he took was **to gather together those who
would lead** the people in celebrating. Not everyone is gifted
to lead. Care must be taken to find the right person or
persons, depending on the occasion.

Levites were the God appointed leaders of the Israelites for
spiritual celebrations. Singers also were brought together.
These individuals had previous training and experience. They
knew what to do in this kind of situation. When people sense
that the one leading them knows what he is doing and is
confident in leading, they more readily follow.

I find this especially true in congregational singing in church.
When the instrumentalist and song leader exhibit skill and
confidence in leading the congregation, the people in the pew
will respond by singing more enthusiastically. They feel as
though the leaders can pull them along so they tend to forget
about themselves and more freely worship the Lord.

The spiritual leaders chosen immediately took an
important step in preparing for celebrating before God the
accomplishment of building the wall around Jerusalem: **they
purified themselves** (Nehemiah 12:30). They knew that
only "he who has clean hands and a pure heart…may ascend
the hill of the Lord…(and) stand in his holy place" (Psalm
24:3-4). They didn't ask the people to do something they

themselves had not done. This was one of the main criticisms
Jesus had of the Pharisees. He declared, "They do not
practice what they preach. They tie up heavy loads and put
them on men's shoulders, but they themselves are not willing
to lift a finger to move them" (Matthew 23:3-4).

In writing of spiritual leaders in the church, Peter explains,
"Be shepherds of God's flock that is under your care, serving
as overseers – not because you must, but because you are
willing, as God wants you to be; not greedy for money, but
eager to serve; not lording it over those entrusted to you, but
being examples to the flock" (1 Peter 5:2-3).

Once they purified themselves "they purified the people, the
gates and the wall" (Nehemiah 12:30). We must be reminded
over and over again that at best we and what we do are
nevertheless unworthy to come into the presence of God.We
might think that doing something significant for God would
suggest that we are okay. But no, we need purifying before,
during and after we do anything for God. And in addition,
what we accomplish must humbly be brought to Him in
prayer for purification. Without the shedding of blood there
is no forgiveness, nor acceptance, by a Holy God. This is
precisely what John had in mind when he wrote
1 John 1:5-10.

Once leaders were chosen and preparations completed **the
actual celebration** took place. A procession was organized

which would give the participants an opportunity to look over the total project even as they celebrated with songs of thanksgiving and praise. Half the people walked the southern half of the wall and the others walked the northern half. At various places along the way they no doubt would be reminded of difficulties encountered and victories won during the building of the wall. Musical instruments and choir voices would burst forth in praise for God's protection, provision and power that enabled them to succeed.

It would be a good practice to memorize hymns of praise so that when we experience God's sufficiency and aid in given situations we would be prepared to worship God spontaneously in song. Such songs subsequently would take on greater meaning to us whenever we sing them because of the experiences they would bring to mind. By relating the experiences to others they too would be enriched when singing with us.

The procession concluded with a glorious celebration in the house of God, the temple. Under the direction of Jezrahiah the two choirs joined their voices in a climactic chorus of thanksgiving and praise. "And on that day they offered great sacrifices, rejoicing because God had given them great joy. The women and children also rejoiced. The sound of rejoicing in Jerusalem could be heard far away" (Nehemiah 12:43).

There is a joy that comes naturally when any task has successfully been accomplished. When the task is done for God's glory and He is praised for having made its accomplishment possible He imparts an even greater joy. It becomes contagious and spontaneous. And it will have far reaching results. That is why we are instructed that in everything we do, we should "do it all for the glory of God" (1 Corinthians 10:31).

This joyous time of celebration was special. It was a spiritual high. But there were **elements of it that were to be maintained** in the life of God's people. Nehemiah didn't wait for some other time to establish that ongoing experience. He set things up while the iron was hot.

"Men were appointed to be in charge of the storerooms for the contributions, firstfruits and tithes" (Nehemiah 12:44). The portions required by the law to underwrite the expenses of the priests, Levites, singers and gatekeepers were to be contributed faithfully. These contributions would be stored and then distributed by these appointed men.

Yes, it costs money to do the work of God. Too often we are ready to give of ourselves and our resources to complete a given project for God. Then, when it is accomplished, there is a tendency to feel we have done our part and to ignore the ongoing expenses for the ongoing work.

Churches need to keep this in mind when they go into a building project. There is a certain momentum and euphoria which grows as a building rises. People will give sacrificially to see the project completed. And times of celebration following its completion are entered into and enjoyed by all. But increased expenses to maintain the building and support personnel for the enlarged ministry often present a problem. This follow-through need must become an integral part of both the project and the celebration of its completion. Only then will the celebration continue as a vital part of the life of the people.

Meditating on the description of this dedication celebration led by Nehemiah has helped me see a weakness in my life. It also has given me guidelines to follow so that I can creatively and spiritually celebrate both what I and others accomplish for God. I am confident this will bring glory to God.

When it was time to celebrate the 25th anniversary of our church and my service as the Founding and Senior Pastor, my wife and I gathered a team who worked at making the preparations for it. Saturday night we had a beautiful banquet at which people who had served in worship led us in songs of praise, others reminisced by sharing significant past experiences and some guests brought words of congratulation. Then on Sunday morning we had a worship service outside to accommodate everyone. The elements of the service were similar to the Saturday night gathering, but with different people participating. My children shared in these gatherings as well. Everyone was inspired and encouraged as we celebrated crossing this milestone in the life of our church.

Afterward I reflected on how this celebration was similar to that of the Israelites in Nehemiah's day. Pictures have captured the event for future generations. I'm sure glad I learned this lesson of celebrating accomplishments before our 25th anniversary and I believe God was glorified as we rejoiced together in His presence.

Application Assignment

1. What was your last major accomplishment?
2. Did you do anything special to celebrate this accomplishment? If yes, list any of the elements touched on in the last chapter that were a part of your celebration.
3. Are you engaged in an important project now? If yes, think of an appropriate way to celebrate when the project is accomplished; a way in which God will be glorified and those who participated affirmed.
4. Have you recently observed someone else or a group accomplish an important task? Did you rejoice with them? Did you do anything special to celebrate their accomplishment?
5. Can you recall a recent celebration that you either observed or participated in which you felt confident brought glory to God? Describe it.

Chapter 5
HANDLING INSPIRATIONAL HIGHS WISELY

Inspirational highs are hard to handle.

Mountain top experiences often hinder the development of stable, spiritual maturity. It's true, inspirational highs produce great spiritual excitement. You see things you have not seen before. It's exhilarating.

Visions often are born on the mountain top. But that just might be why many visions are not carried out subsequently.

You see, seldom can you stay on the mountain top. And the only way to go is down. When you go down, it's hard to maintain the inspiration of that moment and flesh it out in the nitty-gritty experiences of daily life. Being a wise leader during times of inspirational highs requires a number of characteristics difficult to develop and harder to maintain.

I must admit my high estimate of Nehemiah as a leader was tarnished some as I meditated on his description of the spiritual experience of the people of God following the completion of rebuilding the wall around Jerusalem (Nehemiah 8 and following). I realized also how often these characteristics are lacking in my life.

Things had calmed down following the rigors of building the wall. The Israelites settled back into their towns and the normal routines of life. Was this an appropriate time for challenging them spiritually? The seventh month was approaching, a month for celebrating in the religious calendar of Israel. How should they celebrate?

It is not clear whether Nehemiah was thinking about this. Nor is it clear that Ezra was. The account reads, "All the people assembled as one man in the square before the Water Gate. They told Ezra the scribe to bring out the Book of the Law of Moses" (Nehemiah 8:1). It seemed strange to me that the people were taking the initiative and the leaders were followers. Why?

I went back and reread the first seven chapters of Nehemiah to see if Nehemiah had prepared the people for such an initiative. All I found was his own call, the sharing of his vision and the many times prayer was introduced to overcome opposition during the building project. Not once was it suggested that Ezra read God's Word to the people. Nor were they encouraged to meditate upon it.

Was the building project too urgent? Were they too busy during the project to do it? Was it necessary to get the wall built that fast?

I wondered if after the wall was completed and they were back to "things as usual," they sensed something missing. At first they didn't know what. Finally they thought that God's Word might give them some answers.

I know this is arguing from silence. But leaders among God's people should **take the initiative in cultivating an interest in God's Word and seeing to it that it is clearly understood and carefully followed.**

Getting back to Nehemiah's account, it was interesting to me on the positive side to see how readily Ezra responded to their request, surely with Nehemiah's full consent. A pulpit was built. The Book of the Law was brought. And at sunrise the book was opened. All the people stood. In preparation for reading "Ezra praised the Lord, the great God; and all the people lifted their hands and responded, 'Amen! Amen!' Then they bowed down and worshiped the Lord with their face to the ground" (Nehemiah 8:6). Ezra read the Law aloud and the people listened attentively from daybreak till noon. Interspersed with the reading by Ezra the Levites instructed the people, "making it clear and giving the meaning so that the people could understand what was being read" (Nehemiah 8:7-8).

It is clear that Ezra and the Levites were prepared to respond to the people's request and readily did so. It is clear by the context that Nehemiah also was positively involved. As leaders they were spiritually in tune and willing to share what they knew, though the people had taken the initiative. This takes **humility**, also a key characteristic of leadership.

Something many leaders lack is **sensitivity.** Nehemiah was sensitive in detecting danger. He was also sensitive to God's work in his own life. But as is true with many strong-driving, goal-oriented leaders, he was not always sensitive to what God was doing in the lives of others, nor patient enough to allow the time required for God to finish each phase of His work in their hearts.

As God's Word was read and explained to the people, it cut deeply in conviction resulting in their mourning and weeping. To Nehemiah, Ezra and the Levites this response was not appropriate. They felt that a day which was sacred to the Lord should be celebrated with joy. "Go," Nehemiah declared, "and enjoy choice food and sweet drinks, and send some to those who have nothing prepared. This day is sacred to our Lord. Do not grieve, for the joy of the Lord is your strength" (Nehemiah 8:10).

In Susa, not many months before, when Nehemiah heard about the conditions in Jerusalem, he sat down and wept. In fact he mourned and fasted and prayed before God for some days (Nehemiah 1:4). Could it be that he now pre-empted the working of Godly sorrow in the lives of the Israelites by introducing the need for joyous celebration prematurely?

The Feast of Tabernacles was to be a time of rejoicing, but that was to start in the middle of the month. Why not let sorrow, growing out of exposure to God's Word, do its full work? "Repentance that leads to salvation and leaves no regret" (2 Corinthians 7:10-11).

Jesus describes the process as follows: "I tell you the truth, you will weep and mourn while the world rejoices. You will grieve, but your grief will turn to joy. A woman giving birth to a child has pain because her time has come; but when her baby is born, she forgets the anguish because of her joy that a child is born into the world. So with you: Now is your time of grief, but I will see you again and you will rejoice, and no one will take away your joy" (John 16:20-22).

I remember visiting a Bible school in France where the Spirit of God broke through in convicting power. The first day it happened I had concluded my comments by sharing some reports of revival breaking out in a number of Christian schools in America. I closed a few minutes before the bell to close chapel and suggested that we have a time of prayer. Immediately someone prayed fervently, followed by others who prayed with brokenness and intensity. When the chapel bell rang the students were promptly dismissed. I was disturbed and suggested to the director of the school that if

the Spirit was working the next day that we be open to
extending our time with God beyond chapel.

The next day I again shortened my message to give time for
prayer. At first it seemed as though nothing unique was going
to happen. Then as the time for the bell approached a student
from Madagascar, who within months was to graduate and
enter Christian service among his people, rose and went to the
front of the gathered assembly. Humbly, through tears, he
confided, "I have been examining my heart recently and now
have concluded that I never have been saved. I here and now
accept Christ as my Savior and Lord. Please pray for me."

His confession and request for prayer was electrifying. After
a few prayed someone else got up and confessed a critical
attitude and asked forgiveness. Again after a few prayed
another rose and confessed something he was convicted
about.

This continued for about five hours with many confessing
various sins about which they were convicted. Periodically
the director of the school got up and suggested that maybe
some of the critical feelings they were confessing were
justified and cautioned them not to get up just because others
had. Almost every time he did this another student would get
up and through tears confess his or her critical spirit. Other
sins were also confessed, some seemingly minor, others
rather serious.

When sufficient time had been given for Godly sorrow to do its work, the spirit of the group turned to joy and singing and praise. I am confident many who participated in that time were never the same.

It takes time for fallow ground to be broken up. **Leaders must be sensitive to what God is doing and let the full process take place.** Otherwise we might short-circuit the perfect work of God.

This, however, does not mean that the people of God cannot have meaningful, even joyous, deeply moving experiences. In fact, the next day the men came back to hear more from Ezra. As the Word of God was read, details about preparations for the Feast of Tabernacles became clear. Swift obedience followed. And according to Nehemiah's account there had not been a comparable celebration of this feast from the time they first occupied the land under Joshua until then. They celebrated with enthusiasm, devotion, and much joy.

Later the same month they called a solemn assembly at which time they worshipped, confessed sin, renewed their devotion to God and pronounced a solemn vow affirming their determination to follow God and further His cause wholeheartedly (Nehemiah 9:1-37). All the leaders,beginning with Nehemiah, signed the vow (Nehemiah 9:38-10:39).

The record suggests that as long as Nehemiah was there to see that the vow was carried out, everyone stayed true to their commitment. At least outwardly. But as soon as he returned to his job as cupbearer to the king in the city of Susa, the people remaining in Jerusalem softened, compromised, and sinned against God by breaking virtually every vow they had made. Tragically their commitment was shallow and short-lived.

Why? What caused this spiritual and moral collapse?

Did Nehemiah lack discernment regarding the genuineness of their response to truth and conviction? Was he too anxious in accepting their profession as genuine? Does a leader have the responsibility to challenge the genuineness of someone else's response?

There is a place for idealism in leaders, but never at the expense of realism and authenticity. When Joshua stood before the Israelites he challenged them to choose whom they would serve. When they indicated they would serve God he questioned their sincerity (Joshua 24:14-28). He pressed them to examine themselves.

Jesus did the same. When the crowds started turning away from Him He asked His disciples, "You do not want to leave too, do you?" (John 6:67).

He explained the implications of their response many times during their time with Him and asked them to reevaluate. When they did He affirmed and encouraged them.

When Nehemiah returned to Jerusalem some time later and found the sad conditions resulting from the people's compromises, he again took things into his own hands. He demanded reforms. He forced compliance. He ruthlessly pulled it all together again.

But there is a question that remains in my mind and heart. Were the people's hearts in the reforms? Or was there compliance, like that of the little boy who was made to sit in the corner for punishment but who said to himself, "My heart isn't sitting down!"

Application Assignment

1. What would you consider to be your greatest inspirational high? What initiated it? Were there any permanent results in your life?
2. Can you think of a time when someone interrupted a work of God in your life? What was the effect on you?
3. Can you think of a time when you feel you might have interrupted a work of God in someone else's life? What would you do differently if the same situation came up again?

4. Have you ever sensed that the response of a person or group was shallow and should have been examined more thoroughly? How could you have done this and still encouraged them to go on making a deeper and more mature response?

5. What can a leader do to make the people he leads able to stand and go forward in their spiritual walk even when he is not present to check up and/or correct because of other demands on his life?

6. What is the proper place for "godly sorrow" and/or "joy" in the life of the Christian?

IN CONCLUSION

Obviously this has been a brief treatment of the subject of **leadership** and of the example of Nehemiah. He accomplished great things for God. He demonstrated many important principles and guidelines which enabled him to succeed as he did. But he was not perfect.

If we can learn from him how to take the initiative, and having taken it, how to creatively persevere until a goal is reached we will have benefited greatly. All of us will face opposition along the way. We need to develop a response strategy to overcome intimidating individuals or situations as Nehemiah did. But we need to be careful that we are building strong, consistent character in the lives of those with whom we work and live and lead. That's what really counts.

As I think back on my parental responsibilities with four children, I realize that things didn't just fall into place automatically. My wife and I had to have goals in mind as we related to our children and trained them in the way they should go. As they got older we needed to find new ways to relate to them so that we continued to have a positive influence on them.

Guidelines for living needed to be instilled early in life and reinforced throughout their growing years. They needed to see them exemplified in our lives as we made decisions day by day. But they needed to be explained as well so they could understand the why and wherefore. This would help them implement the principles when they were on their own.

Independent responsible living must be encouraged. Not so that children will not want to have anything to do with their parents. But so they would not be crippled when faced with making decisions when their parents weren't around. That is the only way they would become strong and mature enough to be able to do the same with their children when they had a family.

The same basic principle is true of leaders within the church. Our ultimate goal of seeing people come to Christ and grow to full maturity doesn't just happen. It is obviously a work of God (Ephesians 4:11-16).

We therefore need to determine what a mature Christian is and establish that as our goal for everyone who becomes a Christian in and through our ministry. For this to happen, the leaders must clearly exemplify movement toward that goal in their own lives. They must humbly be able to say with Paul, "Join with others in following my example" (Philippians 3:17), "Imitate me" (1 Corinthians 4:11-16).

Then as an outgrowth of their example leaders are to teach
what spiritual maturity entails and how to grow into it. This
is a long term process and commitment. It requires at least
something of a personal contact between leader and follower.
Paul told the Philippians, "Whatever you have learned or
received or heard from me, or seen in me – put it into
practice" (Philippians 4:9). Some years ago I wrote an article
that presented **Paul's personal management secrets** under
the title, "If Paul got organized, so can you." It is included in
this book as a postscript.

Specific accomplishments related to the ultimate goal are
good, important and fulfilling in themselves. But if the
ultimate goal is not realized they will not really satisfy. Nor
will they bring God the glory He deserves.

Ultimately, leaders need to work themselves out of a job
while equipping others to replace them. Only when their fruit
remains, without being dependent on them, is God's purpose
fulfilled. Let us not stop short of that objective.

Postscript A
Paul's Personal Management Secret
If Paul Got Organized, So Can You

Many of us struggle with the challenge of organizing our lives so we can become who God wants us to be and accomplish what He wants us to do.

The more I have considered this problem, both in the light of my own life and ministry goals, and in the light of Scripture, the more convinced I am that all of us can learn much from the Apostle Paul, who at the end of his life declared, *"I have fought the good fight, I have finished the race, I have kept the faith."* In his mind, Paul had done what God had called him to do. He could share with humble confidence, *"There is in store for me the crown of righteousness, which the Lord, the righteous judge, will award to me on that day"* (II Timothy 4:7-8).

This is not to say that he did not struggle with many of the same issues we wrestle with. But he did have a clear perception of why God had saved and called him into His service. He knew how to manage his life and ministry with a view toward finishing the race. He knew how what he did fit into God's purposes for the church. What was Paul's personal management secret? He gives a glimpse of it in Romans 15:14-33.

Maintaining Perspective

Paul gained and maintained perspective in his work by clearly knowing where he had been, where he was, and where he was going. In other words, he knew what he had accomplished, what he was presently doing, and what he still intended to do in the future.

1. *Where he had been.* Paul's accomplishments were noteworthy (vv. 18-19), through the power of Christ and the Holy Spirit. Gentiles from Jerusalem to Illyricum had come to Christ through what he had said and done. In fact, he said there wasn't a place for any more of his work in these regions (v. 23).

When you get discouraged, it's good to be able to look back and reflect on what God has enabled you to accomplish. Some people keep a file of letters of affirmation and thanksgiving from those whom they have helped. When discouraged, they read those letters for encouragement.

2. *Where he was.* Paul did not suffer from any lack of certainty about his present task. He was on his way to Jerusalem to serve the church there with an offering from believers in Macedonia and Achaia (vv. 25-26). This was not a "Priority One" task with him, but it was part of the big picture of building Christ's kingdom. He was committed

to finishing it and making sure the poor among the saints in
Jerusalem got what had been raised (v. 28).

You can't live on your past accomplishments. When the
going gets tough and confusion sets in, it's okay to read your
appreciation letters; but don't spend too much time on it.
Look to the past for perspective, but don't live in the past. If
you do, you may never complete your present assignment,
especially if it's not "Priority One" with you. Complete your
present task as soon as you get your batteries charged from
your memory file of affirmation and accomplishment.

3. *Where he was going.* While you are completing your
present task, begin thinking about where you will go and what
you will do next. Paul carefully wove his future plans into
his report on what he had done and was doing. He planned to
go to Spain and he hoped to visit the Roman believers on the
way (vv. 23-29). He looked forward to their assistance and
fellowship. Immediately, however, he was en route to
Jerusalem.

Your future might look more exciting than your present, and
in the scheme of things it might be more important. What
you are now doing might have its negative side. Paul's did.
Be careful that you don't start living in the future so much
that you never complete your present assignment. Use your
future plans to motivate you in your present task and help you
maintain perspective.

As you plan for the future, try to reach far enough so it will take God's involvement to accomplish it. But be careful not to reach out so far that your future goal becomes unreachable.

Maintaining Discipline

Paul not only maintained perspective in his life and ministry, he also found a way to maintain discipline to do what God wanted him to do. He established a purpose statement, goal statements, and a list of measurable objectives.

1. *Purpose statement.* Paul's purpose statement was actually taken from Isaiah 52:15 (cf. v. 21). In preaching the Gospel of Christ where His Name was not known, he was fulfilling Old Testament prophecy. Can you state your purpose as clearly as Paul did? If you don't know what it is, you will have a hard time maintaining discipline in your life and work.

My purpose statement for ministry is based on Colossians 1:28, Ephesians 4:11-13, and I Corinthians 9:19. Put in my own words, it is "to equip and encourage others to be and do all God wants, especially those with potential for leadership and those already in positions of leadership".

2. *Goal statements.* Having established his purpose, Paul broke it down into goal statements, so he could rank his activities. First, he wanted to preach where Christ was not known (v. 20). That was such a priority in his life that he put

off other desirable tasks, such as visiting the church in Rome
(v. 22). Reminding himself of his top goal drove Paul when
the going got rough. It helped him maintain discipline in
fulfilling his calling.

Paul also wanted to help new Christians grow, so they could
advance God's kingdom. He knew the Roman believers were
"full of goodness, complete in knowledge, and competent
to instruct one another" (v. 14). Nevertheless, they needed
some reminders (vv. 15-16). He wanted them to be capable
of helping him in reaching the unreached.

I have two primary goals in ministry that are similar to Paul's
second goal. I want to equip, encourage and empower the
believers in our church to do the work of ministry that God
has called and gifted them to do. In addition, I look for
opportunities to encourage those already in ministry in the
church to stir up their gifts and sharpen them for the work
God has called them to do.

Paul's third goal was to see the Body of Christ function as it
should, with each member doing what it was designed to do.
In context, this meant Gentile believers who had shared the
Jews' spiritual blessings would also share their material
blessings (v. 27).

Paul's goals, therefore, were to reach the unreached, to
establish and equip the believers so they could help in the

evangelistic task and to see Christians working together in
harmony and mutual support.

3. *Measurable objectives.* With his purpose and goals in
mind, Paul established some measurable objectives. They
were precise enough so when they were completed he could
check them off as having been done. In this part of his letter,
note what they were:

- Equip believers to be able to do the work of ministry.
  Write a letter to accomplish this (vv. 14-15).
- Saturate one area with the Gospel before reaching out to
  another (v. 19). Since that was finished, he set his sights
  on Spain (vv. 23-24).
- Reach Spain until there was a church there.
- Deliver famine relief to Jerusalem (vv. 25-26).
- Be delivered from unbelievers in Judea (v. 31).
- Visit Rome and get assistance from the church to go to
  Spain (v. 24).

After each of these objectives was reached, Paul could check
them off his list.

Furthermore, it's very difficult to evaluate progress in your
life if you don't have measurable steps you intend to take
toward achieving your goals. It is also difficult to encourage
yourself if you can't see your progress in reaching objectives.

Maintaining Spiritual Dynamic

The Apostle Paul knew how to maintain spiritual dynamic in his life and work. How can you do it?

1. *Make sure what you do is Biblical.* Paul used Scripture to state his purpose (v. 21). What he was seeking to do grew out of the Old Testament promise. Always ask yourself, "What Biblical reason do I have for considering a project or activity?" You will find inner strength from God if what you do has a Biblical foundation.

2. *Make sure what you do is prayerfully undergirded.* Paul pleaded for his brothers to join his prayer struggle (v.30). He knew prayer support was crucial to accomplishing his task. Ask yourself,"Have I prayed over this matter sufficiently? Do I have prayer support from other believers to expect God's blessing?" I have sensed the prayer support of our church more when I am overseas on short-term mission assignments than during my regular church ministry. Likely, this is because I ask for specific prayer when I go on those trips.

3. *You must be a team player.* Paul knew he could not do what had to be done without the help of others. "Join me," he asked (v. 30). He wanted to be refreshed in their company (v. 32). Look at the list of names of people who helped him (Romans 16). They were part of his team. They were

strategic to him and his work. They were either part of a
sending church, a receiving church, or a team sent.

His network of people included men and women, older and
younger Christians, and represented multiple cultures. Mutual
respect, confidence and dependence between all parts of the
international church are increasingly important if the church
is to fulfill its mission.

Conclusion

Paul worked deliberately. Clearly, he knew where he had
been and what he had done. He knew where he was and
where he was going. He had a strong, motivating purpose.
He had clear goals as he moved from place to place. And he
worked hard to complete the tasks and objectives to enable
him to achieve his goals. No wonder he could say, "I have
fought the good fight, *I have finished the race, I have kept the
faith"* (II Timothy 4:7).

I have observed Christians who are doing all of the above.
They are working so hard at it that they have become
workaholics. Paul explained in his letter that one reason he
was planning to visit Rome was to be refreshed (vv. 24, 32).
In organizing your life and ministry, make sure to include rest
time, recreational time, refreshing time, and flex time. All of
us need this balance to be productive. If we would do this,

I believe the result would be less frustration and failure, and more faithfulness, fervency, and fruitfulness, to the glory of God and the building of His Church.

Postscript B
My Biblical Hero's Mentoring Model

As I have read and studied the Bible over the years I have come to the conclusion that Barnabas is the person I resonate with most fully. I consider him to be my Biblical mentor. I have benefited greatly from studying how he ordered his life and impacted those around him.

Barnabas was an ordinary, Jewish businessman from Cyprus who first appears on the Biblical scene in Acts 4:36-37. In these verses it is assumed that Barnabas (his real name is Joseph), was a convert to Christianity and identified with the burgeoning church in Jerusalem. He was given the name Barnabas because he was always encouraging fellow Christians (the name Barnabas means son of encouragement).

In studying his life it appears that the first step toward becoming a maturing Christian after trusting in Jesus Christ for your salvation would be caring for fellow Christians in a positive, tangible way. Too often indifference or insensitivity toward those closest to us stifles the development of Christian character and influence. The place to start is in your Jerusalem, where you live, by looking for those who have a need and doing what you can to help meet that need.

According to 1 Peter 4:7-11 discovering your gift for service starts with prayer, love for one another and opening up your home and life to others without grumbling. Those who have learned what Paul says Jesus taught, "It is more blessed to give than to receive" (Acts 20:35), have taken the first step toward becoming mature Christians and servant/leaders.

Sometimes you can give more than encouragement. Barnabas owned some property. At one point, after he had offered encouragement to many, he saw the need to go one step further: sell what he had, or possibly just some of what he had, and give it toward the needs of caring for the church and her ministry. It has been said, "The water of life is offered freely to anyone who needs and wants it, but it costs something to make it available."

Often giving what you can materially toward the cause of Christ is another one of those first steps necessary in the cultivation process of becoming a mature Christian. If you can't let go of material attachments you will find it difficult to develop a sensitivity to those around you who don't fit into your own little circle of friends, let alone someone in the next community, state, country or continent. Jesus said, "Where your treasure is, there your heart will be also" (Matthew 6:21). These first steps are steps anyone can take. They demonstrate compassion as you care for those in need around you.

The next time you find Barnabas mentioned is Acts 9:26-28
where he is still doing what he had been doing before, only
now the stakes were higher. Saul the persecutor had become
a Christian in Damascus. Word had traveled fast about this,
but it was very hard for those who had felt the full brunt of
his persecution to believe that he was truly saved. Maybe this
was just another ploy of his to infiltrate the church to find out
who the leaders were.

It took courage, but Barnabas saw a man hurting and in need
of being accepted. He risked his reputation and possibly his
life to go out and meet Saul. He spent enough time with him
to be assured that conversion had really taken place and to
gather information to persuade the believers in Jerusalem that
Saul was now one of them. Becoming a mature Christian
involves believing that God can take anyone in the world and
transform them through the power of the Gospel. If you don't
believe that, it will be virtually impossible to see the potential
of God making an impact on the world through you and what
you do.

Have you ever prayed for someone specifically and then saw
God answer that prayer by bringing the person to faith in
Christ? If not, that would be a good place to focus some
attention and effort. Have you ever reached out to someone
you heard was a new Christian and befriended them and
prayed for them? When you do this and you see them

blossom into growing Christians you will be encouraged to
do it again with someone else. This is how faith grows. It
is also how vision grows. It is a part of becoming a mature
Christian and servant/leader.

As you read further in the book of Acts it is exciting to see
each new advance that the church was making. Some
advances were planned by the leadership in Jerusalem. Other
advances seemed to be spontaneous, and they often had
unexpected results. Some new converts from Cyprus and
Cyrene went to Antioch and shared the good news with
Greeks there (Acts 11:19-21). When they responded to Christ
word spread quickly through the Jewish churches. To make
sure that what was taking place was not heretical, the leaders
in Jerusalem sent (guess who?) Barnabas to check it out.

His natural interest in others gave him an openness and
objectivity in observing what was taking place and when
he "saw the evidence of the grace of God, he was glad and
encouraged them all to remain true to the Lord with all their
hearts." Then Luke adds; "He was a good man, full of the
Holy Spirit and faith, and a great number of people were
brought to the Lord" (Acts 11:23-24).

Exposing yourself to what God is doing beyond your own
circle of believers stimulates faith and vision and cultivates
a world view for the work of God. When you begin to see

what God is doing as well as what the tremendous needs and opportunities are in the world beyond your own comfortable circle of friends you will be gripped with one of two responses. One is that the situation is so huge it is hopeless and you throw in the towel and do nothing. That leads to stagnation and death spiritually. This is true in individual lives as well as in churches.

The other response is that though you realize you can't do it all alone, if you get others to join you, a greater impact for God and His kingdom can be made. Barnabas concluded that what was taking place in Antioch needed to be encouraged and expanded so he "went to Tarsus to look for Saul, and when he found him, he brought him to Antioch. For a whole year Barnabas and Saul met with the church and taught great numbers of people. The disciples were first called Christians at Antioch" (Acts 11:25-26).

No one of us can get the job done alone. No two of us can. But if we keep working at teaming up with others, and they in turn do the same, we can make an increasing impact on our world for the glory of God.

The 11th chapter of Acts closes with the believers in the new church in Antioch rallying to provide financial support for the church in Jerusalem which was experiencing the effect of a time of drought. Growing mutuality among Christians in ministry will develop an appreciation for the whole church in the world and will contribute toward the cultivation of mature Christians.

When Barnabas and Saul returned from Jerusalem they brought John Mark, Barnabas's younger cousin with them (Acts 12:25). While ministering in Antioch the Holy Spirit called Barnabas and Saul to initiate a new forward thrust toward the unreached. They took John Mark with them as a helper. Though Barnabas appeared to be the leader as they left on this first pioneer journey Saul almost immediately took the lead. It appeared to be spontaneous and prompted by the Holy Spirit, and there is no indication that Barnabas was offended or resisted the move. In fact it seemed he encouraged Saul, now called Paul, to take the lead. Again, the mature Christian and servant/leader is one who is not involved in reaching the world with the Gospel for personal gain or recognition. He always realizes that for the world to be reached it will take a team effort, with each team member encouraged to excel in what he is most gifted to do.

When John Mark left them to return to Jerusalem it doesn't appear that Barnabas or Saul tried talking him out of leaving. But as you read on in Acts, it is obvious that Barnabas didn't forget him. After their trip was completed and the church in Antioch sent them to Jerusalem for the first Church council they returned to Antioch and engaged in a ministry of teaching and preaching the word of the Lord.

Once one has experienced the challenge of reaching the unreached the desire to see the church's outreach and influence continue to expand keeps on surfacing. It is not surprising, therefore, to read in Acts 15:36, "some time later Paul said to Barnabas, 'Let us go back and visit the brothers in all the towns where we preached the word of the Lord and see how they are doing.'" Nor is it surprising to read, "Barnabas wanted to take John, also called Mark, with them" (Acts 15:37). If outreach is going to continue expanding it will take more and more workers. Barnabas saw potential in John Mark even though he had deserted them on the first missionary journey. Paul disagreed. As they discussed this "they had such a sharp disagreement that they parted company" (Acts 15:39). Yes, disagreements can get intense even between godly, mature Christians committed to world evangelism.

There is so much at stake when trying to reach the world with the Gospel that those committed to the task feel so deeply about how best to do it that personal differences can become quite intense. There is nothing wrong with creative tension, but when it leads to splits the cause of Christ is hindered. It would have been better had they called the church leaders together, shared their differing views, prayed and fasted, and patiently waited and listened for God's guidance.

It is true, Paul took Silas as a teammate and with the church's blessing started out on a very successful 2nd journey.
Barnabas took John Mark under his wings and left fo Cyprus. In time the breach between Barnabas and Paul appeared to be overcome, but how much better it would have been had they been reconciled and able to joyfully affirm each other as they went separate ways, thus multiplying the potential outreach. God, in spite of their deep conflict, worked His purposes out. But that does not obviate this negative episode.

Barnabas is not mentioned again in the historical record of Acts. We would not know whether he threw in the towel and quit, were it not for a few references to him and John Mark in some of the Epistles. Barnabas discipled John Mark, equipping him to become Peter's side kick as well as one whom Paul later on recognized as being profitable even to him (2 Timothy 4:11). In fact, as John Mark became the writer of the Gospel of Mark, Barnabas, as his mentor, continued to have an impact through him on the spread of Christianity throughout the world. That impact continues down to our present day.

Becoming a mature Christian and effective servant/leader often starts with seemingly small steps of reaching out to help someone in need. Giving toward the support of ministry often stimulates greater commitment. Another trait is keeping your eye open to spot the potential in others and helping them

overcome obstacles in reaching their potential. It's important
to see the task as more important than getting recognition for
your part in it. Responding when called upon to help and
looking for opportunities that come your way are further steps
in cultivating a world vision. Finally, seeing the importance
of reproducing yourself in others to increase the number of
laborers in the harvest field is essential for anyone to become
a mature Christian and effective servant/leader.

Reflecting on my own development as a Christian and
servant/leader there are a number of men who made a
significant contribution to my life. To list a few: evangelist
Johnny Woodhouse, professors Dr. Howard Vos and Dr. Don
Smith, pastors Malcolm Cronk and Al Claasen, and publisher
Kenneth Taylor. The one who made the greatest impact
was my mother. I'm grateful to these and many others who
provided me the encouragement and example I needed. They,
like Barnabas, mentored me.